BIKES

Contents

How It All Began   7
Milestones in Design   20
The Modern Bicycle   26
How the Motorcycle Works   36
Years of Change   48
Bikes Today   64
Racing   76
Glossary   90
Index   92

Published in 1985 by Rand McNally & Company
First published in 1984 by Piper Books Ltd., London
Designed and produced by Piper
Books Ltd., London

Copyright © by Piper Books Ltd.,
1984
U.S. edition © Piper Books Ltd.,
1985

Library of Congress Catalog
Card No. 85–61171

ISBN 0–528–87138–2

Printed in Portugal
by Printer Portuguesa
First printing 1985

BIKES

By Stephen Hoare

Editor: Jacqui Bailey
Designer: David Jefferis

RAND McNALLY & COMPANY
Chicago • New York • San Francisco

How It All Began

People have always wanted to travel at greater and greater speeds. The first bicycles were called "hobby-horses." They were largely used for downhill racing – with no pedals, gears or brakes. This sort of cycling was seen as nothing more than a rather dangerous sport for the young and reckless.

This was also true of the "boneshakers" and "high-wheelers" of the nineteenth century. These bicycles became so fashionable they led to the development of sporting clubs and organized racing. However, only young men could ride these heavy bikes. Cycling was clearly still only a sport for the young and fit.

Bikes For All

The motorized bike marked the beginning of the motorcycle as a practical machine. The first motorcycles were crude machines. They were unreliable and they often broke down. Riders had to be expert mechanics and not mind getting their hands black with oil. But by the early 1920s, motorcycles were heavier and more reliable. They had gears that enabled them to cope with hills. They also had extra power to carry passenger sidecars.

As motorcycles became heavier, bicycles became lighter. The arrival of **pneumatic** tires, gears and reliability made cycling a good means of transport. It provided a new and inexpensive form of vacation – cycle touring.

Racing remained a popular sport. This led to rapid technical improvements. Ultra-lightweight racing machines pushed the cycling speed record ever higher. Motorcycle racing also became a highly competitive sport. The development of the street bikes we have today owes a lot to the search for speed on the race track.

In recent years, however, it is small bicycles and motorcycles that have become more important. As cars have become more expensive and traffic has increased, so bikes are now seen as a cheaper, faster alternative.

The First Bicycle

It is difficult to say who first invented the bicycle because the first two-wheelers were no more than toys. They were something to keep children amused. The first known adult bicycle was called the *Célérifère*. It was designed by a French nobleman, Comte de Sivrac. In 1791, he showed his machine in a Paris park and crowds of people clapped and cheered.

De Sivrac's bicycle was little more than a larger version of a child's toy. The rider sat astride a "wooden horse" and propelled himself along by kicking his feet on the ground.

Within a very short time, riding a bicycle became a fashionable sport in Paris. De Sivrac's machine was renamed the *Vélocifère* and young men used them to race each other in parks or along straight avenues. The avenues needed to be straight because the *Vélocifère* could not be steered.

Above: The *Célérifère* was little more than an adult toy. Its big wooden carriage wheels and wooden frame made it heavy to push and almost impossible to steer.

Leg Power

In 1817, a German inventor, Baron von Drais de Sauerbrunn built a machine whose front wheel could move from left to right. The rider used handlebars to steer the front wheel. Von Drais called his machine the *Draisienne* and it was a great success.

Copies of the *Draisienne* soon appeared in England, where it was rechristened the "hobby-horse." Because the front wheel could be steered, a hobby-horse could be ridden downhill at quite fast speeds with a degree of safety. Even on level ground, speeds of up to 9 mph (15k/hr) could usually be reached with little effort.

There were disadvantages.

The hobby-horse's wooden, iron-rimmed wheels gave a very bumpy ride. The rider's feet would also get covered in mud as he pushed the bike along in wet weather. Within two years the craze had died out. The one or two enthusiasts who continued to ride their machines faced public ridicule.

For the next forty years, cycles were a rare sight on the roads. A few inventors kept trying, however. There are records of three- and even four-wheeled machines which were propelled by the rider in a variety of ways.

The early nineteenth century was a time of rapid industrial progress. New developments in engineering were taking place all the time. It is therefore surprising that it was not until 1861 that the first successful bicycle appeared – sixty years after the first steam-powered locomotive!

Below: Johnson's hobby-horse of 1819 was an English version of the *Draisienne*.

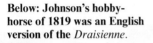

The "Boneshaker"

This breakthrough in cycle design was the *Vélocipède*. Its French inventor, Pierre Michaux, had discovered pedals. The rider's feet no longer trailed along the ground. They were used to turn two pedals fitted to a crankshaft, which turned the axle of the front wheel.

The *Vélocipède* was unusual in other ways as well. Michaux had fitted a simple brake mechanism to the front wheel.

Although Michaux was a coach repairer by trade, he realized that he could make and sell large numbers of *vélocipèdes*. He went into business with his son, Ernest, and the company was soon producing 400 machines a year. Three years later they were able to open a factory employing nearly 300 men.

The *vélocipède*, or "boneshaker" as it came to be known, was an instant success both in the United States and in Britain. Americans regarded cycling as an exciting new sport. Special rinks were built where people could hire a boneshaker for a penny a minute.

In Britain, the possibilities of the boneshaker as a means of transport were shown in 1869. Three men rode 51 miles (83 km) from London to Brighton in under 16 hours.

You had to be strong and fit to ride a cycle, however. Few riders were able to achieve this sort of feat on a heavy machine with no gears. Ernest Michaux, son of the inventor Pierre, had an idea that would help the less energetic. He adapted the *vélocipède* to carry a small steam engine.

Michaux-Perreaux 1869

Below: Ernest Michaux's steam bicycle. The engine was in a dangerous position beneath the saddle. The bike could only travel a short distance before it ran out of steam. It was, however, a serious attempt to produce a motorized bicycle.

Pedal Power

Michaux's original *vélocipède* was a heavy machine. It had a wrought iron frame and wooden spoked wheels shod with iron hoops. The leather seat was fitted onto a springy strip of metal that helped to protect the rider from the discomfort of bumpy roads.

Public demand for *vélocipèdes* was so great that several new companies started to produce them. Each company tried to improve on the design. Wooden wheels were replaced by lighter, metal ones with thin spokes. The rims were shaped to take rubber tires. Hollow tubes were used to make the frame lighter.

Despite cutting down on

weight, however, bicycles were still quite slow. The rider had to make a lot of effort to turn the front wheel. Then it was realized that if the size of the front wheel was increased the bicycle could cover more ground with each turn of the pedal. For the same amount of effort, the rider could travel faster. Wheels of up to 60 inches (152 cm) across were fitted. And as the front wheel got larger so the back wheel became smaller. Its only use, in fact, was to balance the machine. The high-wheeler bicycle was born!

High-Wheeler
The high-wheeler made its first appearance in 1870, but in those days it was known simply as the "ordinary." On a high-wheeler a rider could reach

speeds of more than 20 mph (32 k/hr). But such high speeds brought danger – especially as the machine itself was top heavy. The high front wheel rolled smoothly over bumps and dips in the road, but a large stone could tip up the back wheel and send the rider flying over the handlebars. This sort of accident was called "coming a cropper" and kept a lot of people away from cycling.

Riding in Style

Just above the back wheel was a small step that the rider used to give himself a "leg up" into the seat. If the machine was propped up against a wall, so much the better. Once started, if the bicycle began to fall sideways it could be righted by turning the

Above: The art of riding a high-wheeler bicycle. The front wheel of some models was over 5-feet high.

wheel in the direction of the fall. On the road, there was nothing to stop the rider sailing gracefully along. If he had built up enough speed, he could take his feet off the pedals and put them up on the footrest.

To get off the high-wheeler the rider would skillfully throw his leg over the handlebars and jump down.

Above: A "Sociable" tricycle of the 1890s.

Bicycles Made for Two

In the 1880s, tricycles and quadricycles made their appearance. These larger machines were easy to ride. Instead of balancing on top of a high wheel, all the rider had to do was sit on the machine and pedal. Because of the stability of these machines, a tricycle could also be made to carry two riders.

These tandem tricycles – as they were called – were ideal for both men and women. Soon couples were enjoying leisurely rides. Cycling had become a social activity and not just an energetic sport.

James Starley's Rover Safety Bicycle of 1883 carried the development of the cycle a stage further. On his bicycle, the front and the rear wheels were almost the same size. The Safety's wheels were small compared with the high-wheeler but it traveled just as fast because its rear wheel had gears. Because it was low on the ground the rider could sit astride it without difficulty.

Women in particular became enthusiastic about these more stable bicycles. Although ladies' bicycles had a lower crossbar to allow a skirt to be worn, many lady cyclists preferred to wear divided skirts. These skirts were called "Bloomers."

Below: Bloomers were fashionable for liberated women.

COLUMBIA BICYCLES

It runs Ahead of ALL Other Cycles For LIGHTNESS, STRENGTH, & ELEGANCE.

The First Motorcycles

By 1900, the bicycle was almost a fully-fledged means of transportation. But the motorcycle was still in the early stages of development.

After Michaux, most inventors gave up trying to use steam power. It was too risky for the rider to sit on top of an engine spouting steam, boiling water and flames. In 1876, a gasoline engine had been built by two Germans, Otto and Langen. Their engine ran on a mixture of gasoline and air. As the fuel mixture entered a **cylinder** it was ignited by a spark. This caused a small explosion that pushed a **piston** down inside the cylinder. The piston was attached to a rod, which was, in turn, connected to a wheel, called a **flywheel.** As the piston moved downward it turned the wheel. The movement of the wheel then pushed the piston upward again. This forced the gas from the exploded fuel out through a valve. Then more fuel was pumped in and ignited. In this way, a series of explosions moved the piston up and down, turning the flywheel.

The gasoline engine had many advantages over the steam engine. It was small and compact and ran on a small tank of liquid fuel. The steam engine needed to carry fuel for its boiler as well as water to keep it running. Also, the steam engine needed time to heat up. The gasoline engine could start right away.

A Motorcycle Made of Wood

In 1885, Gottlieb Daimler, a man who had worked with Otto, designed his own gasoline engine and fitted it to a bicycle. Daimler's workshop at Cannstatt in Germany saw the birth

Wilhelm Maybach, Daimler's partner, test drives the *Einspur*. In the same year, in 1885, another inventor, called Karl Benz, fitted his own gasoline engine to a carriage, to make the first gasoline-driven car.

of the world's first gasoline-powered motorcycle.

Daimler called his machine the *Einspur* or "one track." Apart from its engine, the *Einspur* was made out of wood. Daimler bought some wooden carriage wheels and made the frame himself in order to keep the bike a secret from his rivals.

However, despite the fact that the *Einspur* worked well, Daimler never developed his idea further. Instead, he went on to build one of the first automobiles.

The next stage of development was a motorized tricycle. It was built by an English engineer, Edward Butler, in 1887.

Called the "petrol cycle," Butler's invention was a design that paved the way for bigger, faster machines.

When the first automobiles appeared in the 1890s, motor tricycles were very popular. With their tubular frame construction, they were a lot lighter than the motor cars. Tricycles were cheaper and they were faster, too. In the first London to Brighton race, three motorized tricycles, built by the French inventor De Dion, were placed first, second and third.

Compared to cars, though, tricycles did have a few disadvantages. They were exposed to the weather and they were not able to carry more than two people.

A Late Arrival

Motorcycles did not really arrive on the scene until 1896, with the appearance of the Hildebrand and Wolfmüller *Motorrad*. This was the first motorcycle to be commercially produced, and it was a very advanced design. It had a two-cylinder, four-stroke engine (see page 38) that gave it a top speed of 28 mph (45 k/hr).

There was a heavy demand for the *Motorrad* and H&W built a large factory at Munich to cope with the orders. A company was also licensed by them to produce the bike in France. But despite early success, the machine developed a large number of mechanical faults. Customers began to demand their money back. Within a short time, H&W were bankrupt.

The *Motorrad* was a failure because it was too advanced for its time. The first successful motorcycles were a lot simpler. They were no more than push-bikes fitted with small clip-on engines.

Left: The *Motorrad* was the first motorcycle to be manufactured commercially.

Milestones in Design

The first clip-on engine was made by the De Dion Bouton company of France. The Marquis de Dion and his partner, Georges Bouton, were leading names in the early car industry. Their "half a horsepower" ($\frac{1}{2}$ h.p.) clip-on engine was so small that it could be fitted anywhere on a standard bicycle frame. But it was also powerful enough to drive a belt that turned a small wheel, or pulley, that could be attached to either the front or the rear wheel.

The rider still had pedals, however, as a back-up if the engine failed. Pedaling was also necessary to climb a hill. The rider had to share the work of the engine.

Companies all over Europe started copying the De Dion idea. Soon all kinds of motorcycles were seen. One of the best-known early bikes was the Werner. In August 1900, Hubert Egerton completed a journey from the southernmost tip of England, at Lands End, to John o'Groats in the north of Scotland on a $1\frac{1}{2}$ h.p. Werner. The age of motorcycling had arrived.

The Vee Twin

The best place for a clip-on engine was at the lowest part of the frame. This was where the pedals were attached to the frame. An engine in this position made the bike more stable. It helped the rider to balance going around corners. When the engine was sloped forward

Below: A Werner bike, designed by the Russian Werner brothers, with the engine above the front wheel.

Belt

Pulley

Above: American Teddy Hastings, with his 4 hp Indian at the 1907 British 1,000-mile (1,609 km) trial.

or backward along the frame it also helped to strengthen the frame it was fitted to. The sloped engine also allowed room for another cylinder to be added – sloping in the opposite direction. Two cylinders arranged in this "V" shape gave twice as much power and were well-balanced. This type of engine was called a **"vee twin."**

One of the first vee twin engines was fitted to the American Indian motorcyle of 1905. Its power was $3\frac{1}{2}$ h.p. During the next few years, bigger engines were built following the same layout. The 6 h.p. Harley Davidson of 1909 was the first of these big twin-engined bikes.

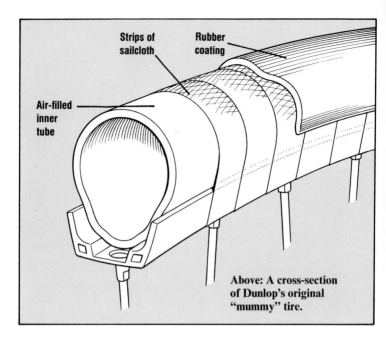

Above: A cross-section of Dunlop's original "mummy" tire.

Pneumatic Tires

Air-filled tires were invented in 1845, by a Scottish engineer, Robert Thomson. They were intended for horsedrawn carriages, but the wooden carriage wheels were too heavy and tended to deflate the tires.

Then, in 1887, an Irish veterinarian by name of John Boyd Dunlop experimented with fitting rubber tires to the wheels of his son's tricycle. He fitted a rubber tube around the wheel and pumped it full of air. The tube was held in place by a long strip of canvas. This was wrapped over the tube and under the wheel rim between the spokes. This cloth covering was then coated in liquid rubber and allowed to dry.

At first, the tires could not be removed for repair. But within two years, detachable cloth and rubber covers had been developed. Dunlop's company went from one success to another. By the last years of the nineteenth century everyone was cycling on the new tires.

Changing Gear

James Starley's Ariel highwheeler of 1870 was the first bicycle to have a gear. But the

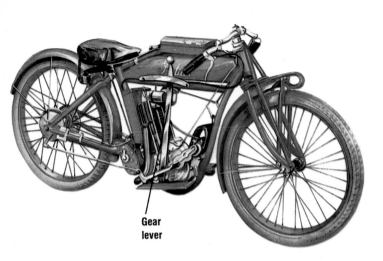

Gear
lever

Above: The 1911 Indian with a two-speed gearbox. Notice the large hand lever at the side of the gas tank.

gears were too clumsy and costly for most people. If people wanted to ride faster for less effort they simply bought a bicycle with a bigger front wheel.

The development of the freewheel in the 1890s marked the breakthrough in gear design. A freewheel allowed the back wheel to keep turning while the chain, which linked the pedals to the back axle, did not. This meant that cyclists could coast downhill without having to take their feet off the pedals. Before the freewheel, the pedals would whizz around at the same speed as the bike's wheels. More importantly, it meant that, by ceasing to pedal, the cyclist could stop the chain and change gear while the bike was moving.

Lindley and Briggs' four-speed **derailleur** gear was developed in 1894, and Johnson's **hub gear** in 1895. Both sorts of gear are in use on bicycles today and are described on pages 27–28.

The first commercial motorcycles were too light to carry the extra weight of a clutch and **gearbox.** But, as bikes got bigger and heavier, gears became essential. The first reliable and effective motorcycle gears were fitted to the 1911 Indian.

23

Some Ideas That Didn't Catch On ...

The development of the motorcycle from its origins to the present day has taken more than a century. As new discoveries were made and tested, performance improved and the shape of motorcycles changed – though not always for the better.

Professor Enrico Bernardi's trailer-cycle dates from 1894. Bernardi couldn't find an engine small enough to fit onto a standard bicycle frame. He made a special trailer for the engine and attached it to the back of the bike. The engine then pushed the rider along. It was an ingenious idea. However, it unfortunately tended to overturn around sharp corners.

The strangest invention of them all must surely have been the mono-wheel. Its American designer, E. J. Christie, boasted that it could reach up to 250 mph (400 k/hr). Like the bicycle, the mono-wheel was based on the fact that a giant wheel could travel a greater distance per revolution than a smaller wheel. But in this case, the fearless inventor sat at the center of the wheel. His weight, above the axle, was balanced by a big 250 h.p. airplane engine fitted below. The engine drove a heavy chain which turned the wheel axle.

The results of the daring inventor's test drive have not been recorded.

Left: Professor Bernardi's trailer cycle of 1894 – a godsend for the lazy cyclist.

Below: The daredevil inventor on his terrifying mono-wheel.

The Modern Bicycle

The bicycle shown below is a lightweight sports roadster. It is a type of bike that has been popular for many years. It has drop handlebars, cable brakes and a ten-speed derailleur gear.

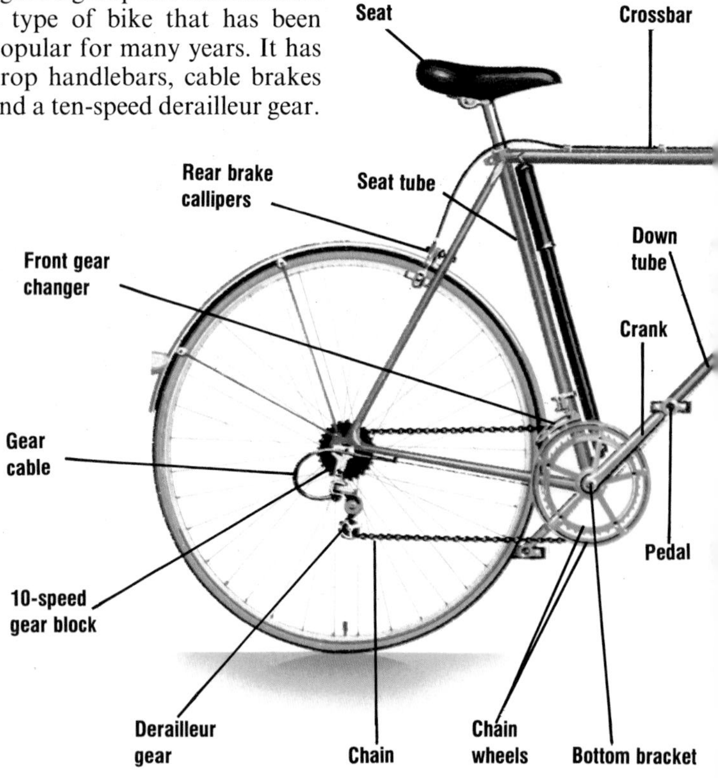

Seat

Crossbar

Rear brake callipers

Seat tube

Down tube

Front gear changer

Crank

Gear cable

Pedal

10-speed gear block

Derailleur gear

Chain

Chain wheels

Bottom bracket

The frame of this bike is made of high-tensile steel tubing – light but very strong. A good lightweight frame can weigh as little as 4 lbs. (1.8 kg). Frames vary in size, so when buying a bike choose one with a frame that allows you to sit with both feet touching the ground on tip toe. The seat can be adjusted to suit your height. The dropped handlebars allow you to crouch while cycling – cutting down wind resistance.

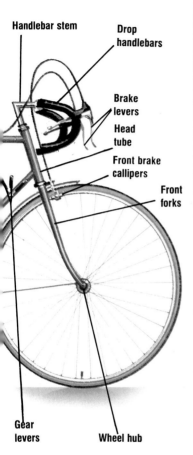

Handlebar stem

Drop handlebars

Brake levers

Head tube

Front brake callipers

Front forks

Gear levers

Wheel hub

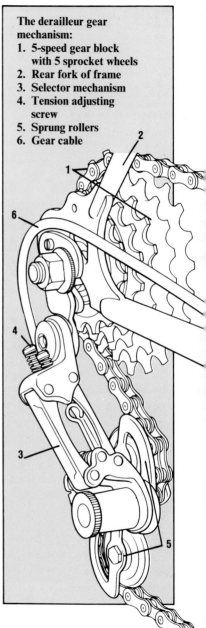

The derailleur gear mechanism:
1. 5-speed gear block with 5 sprocket wheels
2. Rear fork of frame
3. Selector mechanism
4. Tension adjusting screw
5. Sprung rollers
6. Gear cable

The Derailleur Gear

This gear is controlled by a tiny lever on the down tube. It is linked by a cable to the gear selector on the rear wheel. The selector pulls two sprung metal rollers sideways to lift the chain

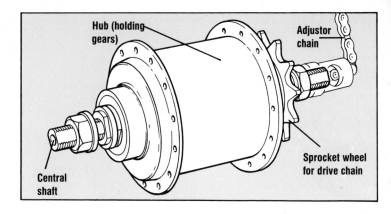

from one **sprocket wheel** to another. The sprocket wheels are built into the freewheel mechanism, and gear changing must be done when the bike is freewheeling.

Derailleur mechanisms can have anything from five to eighteen gears. The number depends on the number of sprocket wheels on the rear **hub** and whether or not the bike has a double **chain wheel.** Double chain wheels are fitted to racing bikes. These have an additional lever on the down tube to operate the front gear changer. This moves the chain from one chain wheel to the other.

Hub Gears

Most hub, or **Sturmey Archer,** systems have three gears housed inside the hub of the rear wheel. A cable connects the gear lever to a small adjustor chain. This is fixed to a sliding shaft that runs through the center of the hub. As the gear lever is moved, the adjustor chain pulls the central shaft backward or forward so that it meshes with one of the three notched gear wheels inside the hub. Alongside the hub is the sprocket wheel. When the rider is pedaling, the drive chain turns the sprocket wheel. This motion is fed through the gears to the bike's rear wheel.

With both types of gear, it is the size of the gear wheels that controls the speed at which the rear wheel turns. In low gear, for example, the rear wheel will turn more slowly than the pedals. This gives more power for hills.

Bike Maintenance

It should not cost much to keep a bike in good mechanical order. With a little time spent in routine maintenance you can avoid expensive repairs later on.

Keeping a Tool Kit
You will need a few basic tools and materials. Your tool kit should contain a combination wrench, a small adjustable wrench, a locking ring wrench, a small screwdriver, a spoke key and tire levers. You will also need rags for cleaning, oil and grease for lubrication, chrome cleaner and a flat repair kit.

Storage
It is important to keep your bike well protected from the weather. Ideally, the bike should be kept cool and dry. If it is not going to be used for a long period, stand it on its saddle to prevent the tires going flat and the rubber from cracking.

Keep the shiny metal parts,

Below: Every cyclist should keep a tool kit for maintenance and repairs. Most bike stores sell a basic kit complete with tool bag.

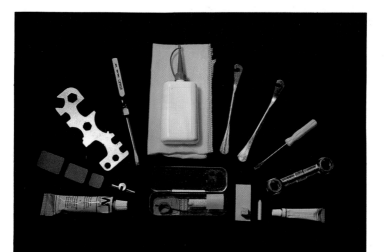

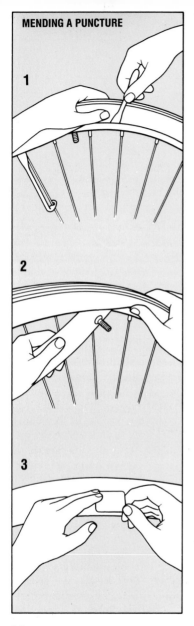

MENDING A PUNCTURE

1

2

3

like the wheel rims and the chain wheel, free of rust with chrome cleaner. Before you take it out of storage, give these parts a light coating of clean oil wiped on with a rag.

Mending a Puncture

Changing a tire or mending a puncture is a fairly straightforward job. Simply take the wheel off the frame and let the air out of the tire. Push three or four tire levers (you can use spoon handles) between the tire and a section of the rim on one side of the wheel **(1)**. As you bend the levers downward, the tire will pop out of the rim. Move one of the levers round the rim to loosen the tire completely so that you can remove the inner tube **(2)**.

A puncture is often caused by nothing more than a tiny pinhole. The best way of finding the hole is to blow up the inner tube and hold a section of it at a time in a bowl of water. The escaping air will cause bubbles. Once you have found the hole, dry the tube and mark the spot with chalk. Then stick a small patch over it **(3)**.

Aligning the Wheel

Before you refit the inner tube, it is a good idea to check that the wheel is aligned properly. Stand the bike upside down. Refit the wheel and spin it. At

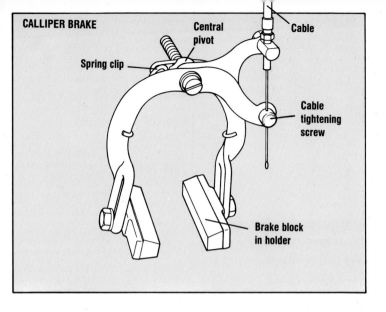

CALLIPER BRAKE

Central pivot

Cable

Spring clip

Cable tightening screw

Brake block in holder

the same time, hold a piece of chalk close to the rim. If the wheel is buckled it will brush against the chalk and leave a mark. To align the wheel, simply tighten the spoke nuts on the opposite side of the wheel from the chalk mark, using the spoke key. Then spin the wheel again and hold the chalk close to the rim as before.

Brakes

Brakes should be checked regularly as your safety depends on them. With cable-operated brakes the callipers should be oiled so that they can move freely. As the brake blocks wear down the cable will need to be shortened. There is an adjustor on each brake lever on the handlebars. This can be used to tighten the cable. It is also a good idea to check that the cable is not loose at the calliper end. By loosening a screw on the calliper the cable can be pulled down and retightened until the brake blocks are almost touching the wheel rim.

To fit new brake blocks, unscrew the holders from the ends of the callipers. Press out the worn blocks with a screwdriver. Put in the new blocks and replace the holders. Then readjust the cable.

31

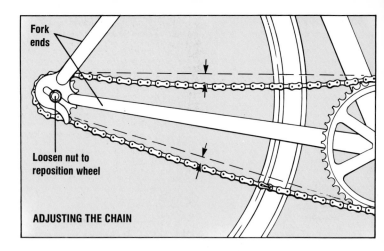

Fork ends

Loosen nut to reposition wheel

ADJUSTING THE CHAIN

The Chain

Check the teeth on the chain wheel and gear sprockets for wear, and check the chain itself. The chain should be adjusted from time to time so that it doesn't become slack. If you can move the middle of the chain up and down by more than $\frac{3}{4}$ in. then it is too loose and needs tightening.

On a hub-geared bike, as shown above, the rear wheel can be moved back in the fork ends to take up the slack. With derailleur gears, the chain is tightened by turning the tension adjusting screw with a screwdriver (see diagram on page 27).

Besides fitting properly, the chain should be kept well oiled. Once a year, the chain should be taken off and cleaned.

Remove the back wheel and slip off the chain. Soak it in a bowl of gasoline and scrub it lightly with a wire brush until clean. Then oil it up again and replace it.

Oiling

There are many parts of the bike that need frequent oiling. A special type of light oil is sold in bicycle stores for this purpose. It comes in a can with a nozzle for squirting the oil onto the parts that need it. Oil the front rear hubs, the handlebar stem, the brake and gear levers and their cables, the brake callipers and the gear change mechanism.

Repairing Paintwork

1. Make sure the area around the scratch is clean and dry.

Then sand the surface smooth with waterproof "wet and dry" abrasive paper, getting rid of any traces of rust.

2. Wipe off the dust with a clean dry cloth. Mask off the surrounding area with newspaper and masking tape.

3. Coat the scratched area with a spray of primer. This protects the bare metal and will allow you to spray paint on top. Wait for the primer to dry before adding the top coat.

4. Make sure you buy a spray that matches the color of your bike. Take off the masking tape. Hold the spray can about a foot from the surface and move the spray slowly and evenly from side to side. Spray on the paint in light strokes. If you hold the spray too long in one place, the paint will run.

When spraying, pick a warm day and do the work outside. Cellulose paint needs heat for it to dry. On a cold, damp day the paint will take a long time to dry. It may also go misty instead of being bright and shiny.

If you are spraying inside a garage or shed wear a face mask. Spray paint can damage your lungs if you breathe a lot in.

REPAIRING PAINTWORK

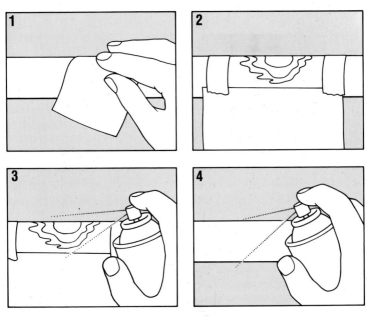

Road safety is very important for cyclists – especially nowadays when roads are full of fast moving cars and trucks. A cyclist should ride close to the curb to allow traffic plenty of room to pass. Parked cars are a problem and the cyclist will need to look behind for oncoming traffic before moving out to pass the cars.

Before taking to the road, a cyclist should learn the rules for driving on the highway. Road signs have to be understood and obeyed. A cyclist must also learn how to make hand signals. All signals are given with the left hand. The right hand controls the back brake so that you can slow down when you are signaling. There are three important signals – arm extended perpendicularly from the body means a left turn; arm extended and raised from the elbow means a right turn; and the arm extended to the left at a 45° angle shows that you are about to slow or stop.

Turning across a line of traffic can be a difficult move. The rider must look behind and, when there is a gap in the traffic, move toward the middle of the road and signal. The arm should be kept fully outstretched so that it can be seen clearly. It should only be lowered when the turn has been made. Right hand turns are no problem, but the cyclist should signal well before the turn and slow down. There may be people crossing the side road.

Equipment

The law says that you must have brakes that work. Your life may depend on being able to stop in time, so check them regularly and replace worn brake blocks.

You must also have good lights. When you ride at night you need to see where you are going and you need to make yourself visible to motorists coming from behind. A bright red rear light on the back wheel and a reflector on the mudguard will make sure that other road users can see you. You can also buy armbands and clothing in bright colors, so that you can be seen on dark and foggy nights.

Finally, make sure your bike is in tip-top condition. A loose wheel or a badly worn chain can bring you to a sudden stop and cause a serious accident. You should be comfortable when riding. If you adjust your seat and handlebars to give yourself a good riding position then you will be able to control your bike better.

DO:
- Watch out for young children and people crossing the road.
- When riding with other cyclists form a single line.
- Watch out for other road users' signals.
- Obey traffic signs.
- Make sure your bike is well maintained and your lights and brakes are working properly.
- Make sure your tires are filled until hard.
- Watch out for car doors being opened.

DON'T:
- Cycle on and off curb
- Carry loads on the handlebars.
- Weave in and out of traffic.
- Ride so fast you cannot stop in time – it takes longer to stop in wet weather.
- Hang onto other vehicles for a tow.
- Swerve suddenly.
- Swing out into the road before turning a corner.
- Ride on sidewalks or footpaths.
- Leave your bike unlocked.

35

How the Motorcycle Works

The motorcycle shown below is a Honda Gold Wing. It is a powerful touring bike and is designed for speed, comfort and safety. It is capable of speeds of over 100 mph (160 k/hr).

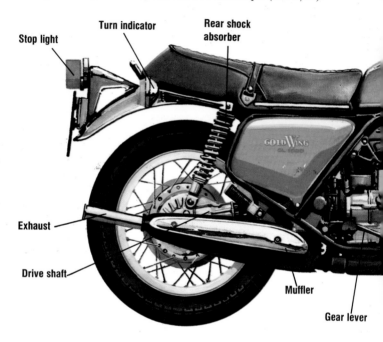

Stop light

Turn indicator

Rear shock absorber

Exhaust

Drive shaft

Muffler

Gear lever

The air-assisted **shock absorbers**, front and rear, cushion the rider against uneven roads. The electronic **ignition** allows smooth running and instant starting.

In front of the handlebars, the road speed and engine "revs" (revolutions per minute) are shown on the speedometer and tachometer. Near the hand grips are switches that control

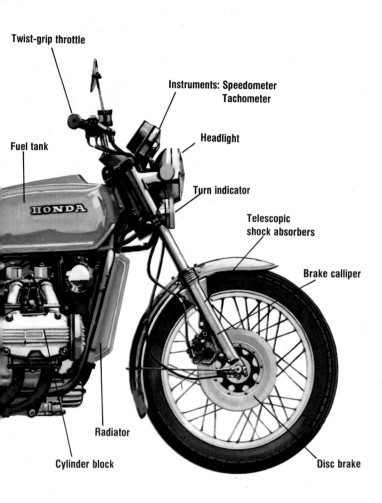

Twist-grip throttle

Instruments: Speedometer Tachometer

Headlight

Fuel tank

HONDA

Turn indicator

Telescopic shock absorbers

Brake calliper

Radiator

Cylinder block

Disc brake

the headlight, indicators, horn and **choke**. There is also a brake lever and clutch lever, plus a twist-grip throttle.

Braking is by disc system – two at the front and one at the back. The engine is liquid-cooled, and a five-speed gear box and **drive shaft** transmit power to the rear wheel.

37

The Engine

Motorcycle engines have between one and six cylinders.

Because of the heat caused by the burning of fuel, engines need to be cooled down. Most bike engines are air-cooled. The block containing the cylinders is covered with fins on the outside that lose heat as the air flows around them. Liquid-cooled engines are surrounded by metal jackets containing water.

A Four-Stroke Engine

Most engines work on the four-stroke principle. The piston has to move four times for each power cycle.

Stage 1 (Intake) The piston moves down and pulls a mixture of gasoline and air through the open intake valve.

Stage 2 (Compression) The intake valve closes and the piston moves up, squeezing or compressing the gas.

Stage 3 (Power) When the piston reaches the top of its travel, a spark from the **spark plug** ignites the gas. There is an explosion, which sends the piston down the cylinder.

Stage 4 (Exhaust) The **exhaust** valve opens. All the spent gases

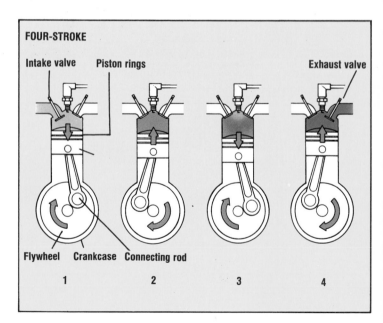

FOUR-STROKE

Intake valve   Piston rings   Exhaust valve

Flywheel   Crankcase   Connecting rod

1   2   3   4

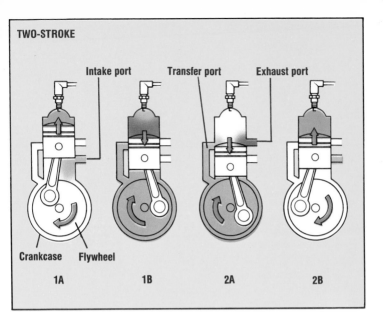

TWO-STROKE

Intake port   Transfer port   Exhaust port

Crankcase   Flywheel

1A   1B   2A   2B

are pushed out of the cylinder by the piston as it rises.

A Two-Stroke Engine

The two-stroke engine only needs an up and a down stroke to complete its cycle.

Stage 1A (Intake/Compression) The piston moves up and opens the intake port. Fuel enters the **crankcase**. At the same time, the rising piston compresses a charge of fuel mixture at the top of the cylinder.

Stage 1B (Power/Compression) There is a spark at the top of the cylinder and the fuel explodes, sending the piston down. The fuel that entered the intake port is compressed in the crankcase, and pushed up into the transfer port.

Stage 2A (Compression/Exhaust) The piston is still falling. When it falls below the exhaust port and transfer port, spent gas escapes and a fresh charge enters the cylinder from the crankcase.

Stage 2B (Compression) As the piston moves up, it begins to compress the charge at the top of the cylinder.

Two-stroke engines are lighter than four-stroke, and because the piston also acts as a valve, they have fewer moving parts to go wrong.

Transmission

The **transmission** is the name given to the system which carries and controls the engine's power to the rear wheel.

The turning power of the engine is passed on (transmitted) from the pistons to the **crankshaft**. Then, by means of a heavy chain or the drive shaft, to the axle of the rear wheel.

But this power is not transmitted directly to the rear axle. There is a gearbox in between. Inside the gearbox there are two shafts – the *input shaft* and the *output shaft*. The input shaft is linked directly to the engine's crankshaft via the clutch. The output shaft is connected to the **drive chain** (or the drive shaft).

The two gear shafts run parallel to each other inside the gearbox and they are linked by gear wheels. The gear wheels on the input shaft mesh with differently-sized gear wheels on the output shaft.

When the gear lever is used to change gear, one pair of wheels is moved sideways and is locked in position. This pair of gear wheels now transmits the engine's power, while the others spin around freely.

The greatest amount of pulling force is given in a low gear. In the gearbox, the lowest gear is the largest wheel and it has the most teeth. In a low gear, the input shaft is turning rapidly, but because the large gear wheel takes longer to make each complete turn, the output shaft will turn more slowly. So although the engine always gives the same amount of power, that power becomes more concentrated in low gear.

In order to change gear, the output shaft has to be disconnected from the input shaft. This is the work of the clutch.

As the crankshaft turns, this movement is passed through the clutch to the input shaft.

When the clutch lever is operated, the springs connecting it to the input shaft are pulled back. This disconnects the input shaft from the crankshaft. While the input shaft is spinning freely, the rider can change gear without jarring the engine.

When the new gear has been selected, the clutch lever can be released. The input shaft is once again connected to the crankshaft and power is transmitted to the rear wheel.

Transmission System:

1. **Air is sucked into the carburetor**
2. **The gasoline/air mixture is ignited in the cylinder, forcing the piston downward**
3. **The piston turns the crankshaft**
4. **This motion passes through the gears**
5. **A chain or shaft carries the power from the gearbox to the rear wheel**
6. **The rear sprocket wheel on the axle turns the rear wheel of the cycle**

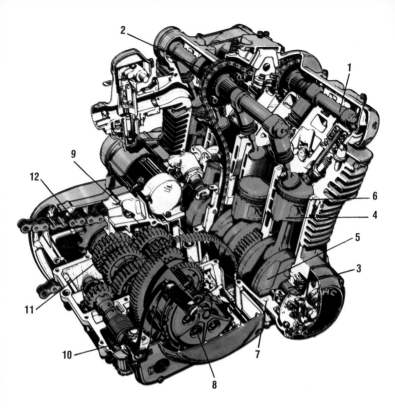

The cutaway drawing above shows the inside of a 750 cc Suzuki four-stroke engine and gearbox.

Shown in green are the double overhead **camshafts** which operate two valves per cylinder (1). The camshafts are driven by a light chain (2) running from the crankshaft – the main shaft (3) that carries the pistons (4) and the flywheels (5).

The piston rings (6) are lightly sprung. They hold oil and form a seal to prevent the exhaust gases escaping from the top of the cylinders into the crankcase (7) below.

The gearbox is shown in blue. The clutch (8) is attached to the input shaft (9). Just behind the clutch is the foot-operated gear lever (10). It moves the gear wheels on the output shaft (11) backward and forward to change gear. At the end of the output shaft is the heavy drive chain (12), which runs to the rear wheel.

The Electrics

The electrics on a bike can either be battery-powered or self generating. Self generating means that the bike has its own tiny generator, or magneto, that creates electric current when the bike is moving. Small bikes are often fitted with magnetos because they can be kick started and they do not need a lot of electricity.

Bigger bikes often have electric starters, powerful lights, a horn, stop lamps and flashing indicators. They also need a high-voltage ignition system to supply current to the spark plugs for several cylinders.

The electric current on a big bike is supplied by a large lead-acid battery. The battery is kept fully charged by an **alternator** that generates electricity when the bike is running.

An alternator is really no more than a magnet that rotates around a coil of wire. It is usually attached to the crankshaft and it therefore revolves at the same speed as the engine. Once the battery is charged, the alternator switches itself off automatically.

Electricity reaches the spark plugs via a **high-tension coil** and a **distributor**. The coil increases the strength of the electric current, which the distributor feeds to each of the plugs.

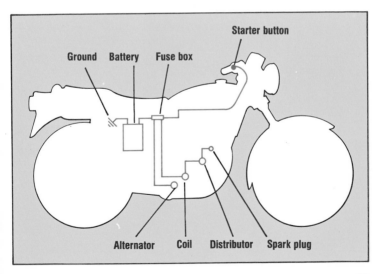

Brakes

A bike must be able to stop quickly, so it is vital to have good brakes. There are two kinds of brakes – **hub** and **disc**. Small bikes do not travel very fast and they are lightweight. Hub brakes are all that is needed to slow down. Bigger bikes have disc brakes for better braking power. High-perfor- mance bikes are often fitted with two front discs as well as a rear disc.

Both types of brake work in much the same way. When the brake lever is pulled, a flat piece of friction-resistant material is brought into contact with the steel hub or disc on the wheel. This slows it down.

Disc brakes are operated by hydraulic fluid. The fluid is kept in a small tank and it

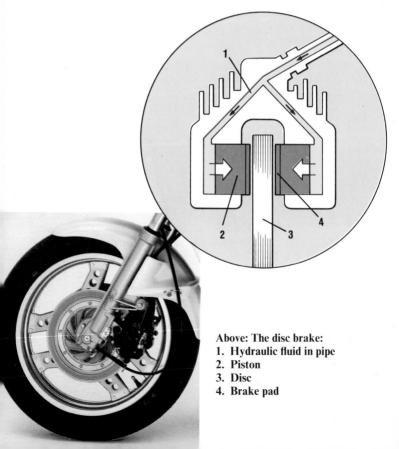

Above: The disc brake:
1. **Hydraulic fluid in pipe**
2. **Piston**
3. **Disc**
4. **Brake pad**

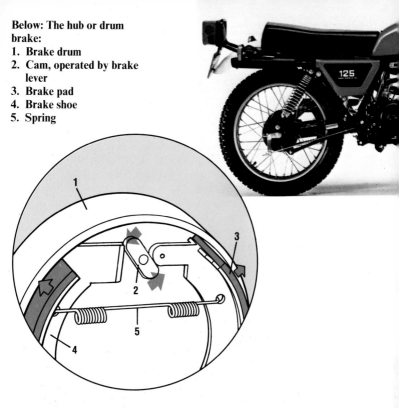

Below: The hub or drum brake:
1. Brake drum
2. Cam, operated by brake lever
3. Brake pad
4. Brake shoe
5. Spring

reaches the brake through a tiny pipe via a master cylinder. The master cylinder is, in effect, a pump. When the rider pulls the brake lever he is actually pumping fluid into the brakes. The hydraulic system is closed and the fluid cannot escape anywhere, so it forces a pair of pistons outward. These pistons push a pair of brake pads against a steel disc in the middle of the wheel, which slows the wheel down.

The hub or **drum brake** is operated by a cable from the brake lever. Inside the drum at the center of the wheel are two curved plates called brake shoes, lined by brake pads. When the brake lever is pulled, it causes a piece of metal, called a cam, to push the two spring-loaded plates apart. The plates move out and the pads rub against the inside of the drum. When the brake is released, the spring pulls the pads back.

Protection for the Rider

Motorcycle riders need special clothing to protect them from the weather and to protect them from injury in case of an accident. All riders should wear a helmet and warm, comfortable clothing helps a rider to concentrate on the road ahead rather than on a draft down the neck!

So let's look at clothing from the feet up. A pair of zip-up fleece-lined leather boots with heavy soles keep the feet warm and are good protection against knocks and scrapes. They are not so good in the rain, though, because water can leak through the zipper. A pair of rubber boots are better for wet weather.

A one-piece nylon oversuit keeps out the rain, but the rider must be warmly dressed beneath it. In winter, long thermal underwear keeps out the cold. Riders who travel long distances need heavier, waxed-cotton clothing. Waxed cotton will keep you warm and dry but it gets dirty easily. Like nylon, it will need reproofing once a year to keep it fully waterproof. For riders with a lot of money to spend, a padded leather oversuit gives excellent protection.

Leathers look good – they are worn by all top racing stars. Leather isn't waterproof, though and motorcycle riders may need a thin nylon oversuit in case of rain.

A rider also needs leather gloves. Hands are the first part of the body to be cut or grazed in a fall.

Helmets

Safety helmets are made from fiberglass or polycarbonate. They do not last forever. If a helmet is dropped on the ground or given a hard knock, it will be weakened. A helmet should be changed at least once every two years. Helmets come in two types – open-face and full-face. The open-face covers the ears and neck and can be worn with or without goggles. The full-face helmet covers the whole head and chin and has a plastic visor.

With the full-face helmet, the plastic visor should be cleaned with a soft rag only. It will scratch easily in any case and should be replaced when it has become too worn. It is not worth trying to save money by hanging on to a scratched visor – your life is too important.

Nylon oversuit with separate jacket and pants

Full-face helmet with visor

Zip-up, padded one-piece leather oversuit

Open-face helmet

Padded gloves

Rubber boots

Leather boots

47

Years of Change

The early years of the twentieth century saw a rapid growth in motorcycle sales as more and more people became able to afford them. Motorcycle and sidecar combinations were popular because they could carry a man, his wife and two children. Road races and reliability trials took place, as manufacturers tried to prove that their bikes alone were the fastest and the best.

Companies such as Indian (1901) and Harley Davidson (1903) in the United States, and Royal Enfield (1901), Triumph (1902) and Norton (1907) in Britain grew rapidly.

War on Two Wheels

In 1914, Europe was plunged into war. In the early days of the war, most armies still relied on horse power. Some regiments went into battle on horseback and horses were used to pull carts and heavy guns. But horses were costly to feed and difficult to replace if wounded or killed. Soon, cars were being used to carry officers from place to place and trucks and buses transported the troops.

Motorcycles had their uses, too, since a dispatch rider on a motorcycle could ride at speed over rough ground, dodging the enemy's bullets. In this way, messages were passed quickly from one part of the battlefield to another.

Special motorcycle and side-car combinations were built to carry machine guns. Although they did not see much action in battle, these vehicles were fast and maneuverable. They could keep pace with moving targets. While the rider steered the bike into position, the machine-gunner aimed his gun and fired.

Above: The Canadian Cyclist Corps.

The bicycle also had its part to play. Soldiers on bicycle moved faster than on foot. When troops had to move quickly from one place to another and trucks were not available, they could be issued with bicycles.

At war, bikes were tested as never before. They had to stand up to tough conditions and work in all weathers. They were built as quickly and as cheaply as possible. Shortages of labor and materials meant that manufacturers had to cut costs by using mass-production methods. By the time peace finally came, factories did not forget the hard lessons they had learned – mass production was here to stay.

Left: Two dispatch riders take a break. Thousands of these Douglas bikes were supplied to the British Army.

49

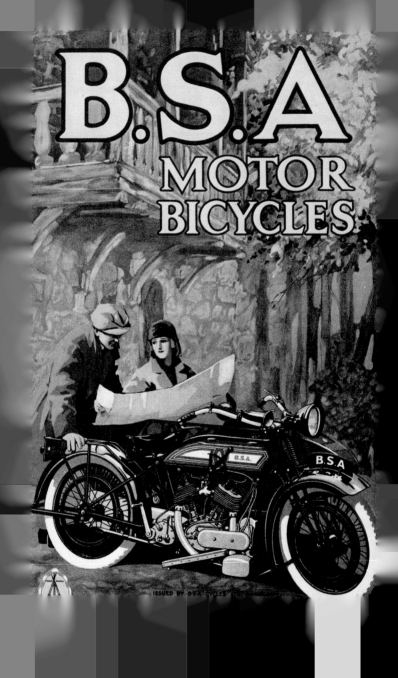

Peacetime Pursuits

After the war, companies were quick to return to producing bikes for peacetime use, but most people had little money to spend. Some firms reacted by producing cheap, lightweight scooters. These experimental machines were very unreliable, however, and the idea was soon abandoned.

Most motorcycles were bought by people who could not afford a car but who needed some form of transportation. Motorcycle and sidecar combinations continued to be popular and as the bikes got bigger, so did the sidecars. Eventually, sidecars offered almost as much comfort as a small automobile. Closed in from the weather, the passenger had a comfortable seat and plenty of leg room.

The after-effects of the war were followed in the late 1920s by a time of depression and unemployment. Industries all over the world were hit badly. In America, the motorbike industry fared badly. Cars were much cheaper because they were mass produced. There were also many second-hand cars for sale. Even many of the poorest families could afford a battered Model T Ford to carry themselves and their belongings around the country in search of a job.

In other countries, such as Britain, the motorcycle industry kept going because it was able to export bikes to countries of the Empire – Australia, Canada, New Zealand, and South Africa.

Changes in Design

However, in spite of the lack of sales, the 1920s saw great days in motorcycle design. Most bikes were built with three-speed gearboxes as belt drives gave way to chain drives. As engines got bigger, so frames had to be made stronger to take the weight. Often, though, the engine was too powerful for the frame and many bikes were hard to handle at top speed.

In 1923, the German company **BMW** (Bavarian Motor Works) launched a bike that was way ahead of its time. Their 500 cc machine had a **flat** twin engine (with the cylinders lying across the body of the bike

Left: A BSA motorcycle and sidecar combination of the 1920s.

51

instead of in line with it). It also had a drive shaft instead of a drive chain. BMW bikes have kept these features to this day.

The new Italian company Moto Guzzi also made an impact. Their small 250 cc machine achieved a record speed of over 60 mph (101 k/hr) at the Isle of Man TT in 1926. It had an overhead camshaft and a gearbox in line with the crankcase.

Cycling for Pleasure

Despite the range of motorcycles on sale, however, many people still could not afford them. Bicycling was a more popular form of transport. In the 1920s and 30s, there were many cycling clubs and young people would often go on

Below: Bicycle touring in Scotland – a vacation snapshot from the 1930s.

vacations on their bikes. The American Youth Hostels were established in the early 1930's. In these hostels cyclists and walkers could find a cheap bed for the night. Hostels are still operated today.

It was also possible to take bicycles by train to faraway places. In the days before cheap air travel and package vacations, cycling held the key to adventurous travel.

Bikes at Work

In the 1920s and 30s, horse-drawn transport was still common in city and countryside. For small loads, though, there was nothing to beat the bicycle, and bikes were adapted to a variety of uses. Delivery bikes were made with a small front wheel which allowed room for a metal holder above it to carry boxes.

In those days, trades people delivered their goods to your door. Milk was also delivered, but not in cartons or bottles. It came in a churn – just as it left the farm. The customers brought their own jugs and the milkman filled them with milk. For loads like this, the delivery bike would have two front wheels to support the load on either side, like a small cart (see above).

Bigger and Better

150 mph (241.9 k/hr).

Speed was an obsession of the 1930s and various riders set out to capture the world speed record. In October 1936, the German rider, Ernst Henne,

Motorcycles of the 30s grew larger and more powerful. Frames became stronger and tires fatter as bikes were built for high performance. Gear changing was revolutionized and instead of a large hand lever at the side of the gas tank, the lever was foot-operated. This allowed quicker gear changing, with throttle and clutch being controlled by the hands.

A number of four-cylinder engines appeared. One of the most successful of these was the Ariel Square Four. This British machine had a 600 cc engine with four vertical cylinders arranged in a square. The engine had two separate crank-shafts and was a great success.

One of the most famous big bikes of the 30s was the 1937 British 1000 cc Vincent HRD. It had an overhead valve, vee-twin engine. And it had a special spring frame and tele-scopic shock absorbers above the rear wheel.

A version of the 1000 cc Vincent, called the *Black Lightning,* broke the U.S. speed record in 1948, when it reached

covered one kilometer at an average speed of 169 mph (272.2 k/hr) on a supercharged 500 cc BMW. Britain's Eric Fernihough, riding a 996 Brough Superior, challenged him and raised the record to 170 mph (273.25 k/hr) the following year. Henne, on a streamlined BMW, replied to this by pushing the record up to 174 mph (279.5 k/hr).

Below: The Vincent HRD was the superbike of the 1930s and 40s. It had a top speed of over 100 mph (160 k/hr) – a performance that would do credit to many modern bikes.

At War Again

Britain and Germany, however, were soon engaging in battles of a different kind as war was declared on September 3, 1939.

Once again, motorcycles played their part in war. Unlike World War I, which was mainly fought from fixed trenches, World War II demanded greater speed as armies moved from one country to another. The German Army, in particular, used motorcycles with machine guns mounted on sidecars. These escorted fast-moving troop trucks as they swept through Europe. The Allied Armies also used bikes to escort convoys of trucks and to carry messages. American forces used more than 300,000 bikes built by Harley Davidson and Indian.

One ingenious development of the motorcycle was a tiny foldaway bike that could be dropped with its rider by parachute. When Allied troops were dropped behind enemy lines, they brought their own means of escape with them!

Right: A German Panzer Corps motorcycle and sidecar was a deadly combination,

The Post-War Years

Above: A scene from *The Wild One* – **the film that made motorcycle riding glamorous.**

At the end of the war, European industry was in ruins. The job of rebuilding bombed houses and factories had to be tackled.

Britain had not suffered as badly as some countries, but it took many years to get back to full production. Many firms were unable to afford the high cost of modernizing their factories. In later years a number of firms had to close down because they could not keep

58

up with the changing modern world. British motorcycles still depended largely on sales abroad.

A New Breed

Many export bikes went to America where, in California, there was a craze for buying big British bikes. California was known as the Motorcycle State and large gangs of bikers took to the roads.

In 1947, a small race meeting at Hollister, California, turned into a battleground when 3,000 bikers descended on the small town and started to run riot. The police were outnumbered and could not stop the fighting. A lot of it was just high spirits, however. The story of that memorable day was told in a film called *The Wild One,* starring Marlon Brando and Lee Marvin. From then on, motorcycles came to stand for freedom and independence. They were a powerful symbol of manhood and aggression. Few girls ever rode with the motorcycle gangs and those who did were passengers.

The most famous gang of all was founded in San Bernadino, California, in 1950. The Hell's Angels were a gang of outlaws whose only possessions were their bikes – everything else they stole.

Above: Factory workers cycling to work in the 1950s.

Gangs in the United States gave biking a bad image, but in Europe the average rider was an ordinary working person who needed a cheap way to get to and from work. If bikers joined a club, it was mostly to talk about bikes and exchange tips on how to repair them.

In the 1950s, many more bicycles, too, were seen on the roads than are seen today. Factory workers needed them to get to work and children used them to ride to school. Few people had cars and often a bike was the only alternative to walking. In cities such as Amsterdam in Holland, bikes are still the main form of transport and many of the city's narrow streets and canal bridges are closed to cars.

Small is Beautiful

When Italian designer Corrado d'Ascanio built a motor scooter in 1946, it was the dawning of a new age. He gave his scooter the name "wasp" – Vespa. Since then, the Piaggio company has built more than five million Vespas.

The post-war world needed small, light, economical machines that could be ridden easily by both men and women. Surprisingly, d'Ascanio's design has changed little over the years. The headlight has moved up beneath the handlebars. There is more luggage space and, of course, some technical improvements have been made.

The strong point about the scooter design was the small, enclosed engine and a direct shaft drive. The engine was behind the rider and it was not only quiet but clean. Other companies were quick to copy the design, and soon Vespa and Lambretta scooters were selling all over the world.

Japan, too, was quick to see the need for small bikes. The little Honda C50 Moped was first made in 1958. Since then, millions of these bikes have been sold worldwide.

As sales of small bikes went

Above: The successful Vespa motor scooter of 1946. It was light, easy to ride and cheap to run. The basic design has changed little in over 30 years.

up, sales of big bikes fell. As soon as people became better off they switched from motorcycles to cars. Cars could cover long distances in comfort and carry all the family. But they were not so useful in towns or for short distance travel. Small bikes were ideal for short distances. They did not use up so much gasoline and they could be parked easily. Some people had a car *and* a small bike.

The Portable Bicycle

In the same way, bicycling was revolutionized in 1957, when a British designer called Alex Moulton invented an entirely new bike. The Moulton had tiny 16-inch (40-cm) wheels, slim tires and a low, open frame. Many people thought it would not go as fast as an ordinary bicycle, but they were wrong. Its big chain wheel and high gears made the Moulton's performance very lively and its rubber **suspension** helped it over bumpy roads. The new bike quickly became fashionable for town and shopping trips. The designer even developed a version of his bike that could be folded away inside the trunk of a car.

Below: Alex Moulton's revolutionary small-wheeled bicycle. At first, he produced them himself. Then the Raleigh company bought his design.

The Rising Sun

In the mid 1950s, there were more than 80 Japanese motorcycle manufacturers. Competition was very fierce and only the fittest companies survived. But those that did grew to be giants. By the 1960s, there were only four left – Honda, Yamaha, Suzuki and Kawasaki.

From the start, these companies realized that if they were going to join the top league bike producers of the world they had to enter teams for the World Championship races. Honda arrived first, and in the 1961 season, came in on top of the

125 cc class and won first, second and third places in the 250 cc championship.

The smaller-engined Japanese bikes were extremely fast and very well engineered. Honda was quickly followed onto the racing circuits by Suzuki and Yamaha. They all had great success. Their fast two-stroke engines quickly made them champions of the 50 cc, 125 cc and 250 cc classes.

Racing success had an immediate "spin off" in the sales of road machines. The small Japanese bikes were ideal for

Left: The little Honda C50 Moped is still basically the same design today as it was in 1958. This bike has sold in millions all over the world.

ing, indicators and efficient shock absorbers.

During the 1960s many motorcycle manufacturers went out of business. Some companies tried to make the big bike more economical to produce. They used standard parts that would fit a number of different machines. This also made it easy for owners to repair their bikes. But those people who did want big bikes were not interested in such practical things as ease of repair. They wanted style – and this is what the Japanese bikes gave them.

The largest market for big, powerful bikes was in the United States. In the 60s and 70s, it imported a lot of big bikes from Britain; but even this market was not enough to save the last major British company, Triumph. It finally closed down in 1983. A few European companies, like Moto Guzzi and BMW survived by concentrating on quality bikes. They paid a lot of attention to design and rider comfort.

beginners to ride. They were easy to handle, and cheap to run. As Japanese bikes penetrated the U.S. and European markets, so they began producing bigger machines as well. By the late 1960s, Japanese bikes were also competing in 500 cc world championships.

A Declining Market

From the 1960s on, big bikes became steadily less popular. The big bikes of the 50s and 60s were noisy and uncomfortable. They did not have such things as electronic ignition, full **fair-**

Bikes Today

Honda MB50

Kawasaki KE125

Most of the world's bikes today are produced by a few companies. But there have never been so many different sorts of bike to choose from.

No longer is the bike a poor relation of the car. A top touring bike will give you comfort, safety and high performance. Add to this the enormous increases in the cost of fuel. This has caused more and more people to switch from cars to bikes.

Many street bikes have been adapted from off-road scrambling machines. These are ideal for young riders because they are suited to relatively low speeds. Sports mopeds, in particular, are very popular. They have all the features of much bigger bikes but at less expense. The Honda MB50, for example, is a full-sized bike with alloy wheels and a front disc brake. It has a two-stroke 49 cc engine and its five-speed gearbox gives it added performance.

Honda VF400

While the MB50 is a street machine, the Kawasaki KE125 is definitely an off-road bike. Its block-tread tires and 10-inch (25-cm) ground clearance are suitable for trail riding, as are its extra long, telescopic **front forks**. The Kawasaki's 124 cc engine has a wide spread of power, and smooth acceleration. This is helped by a five-speed gearbox.

For the experienced rider there are a lot of good lightweight machines under 500 cc that give all the power and performance of the bigger "superbikes." Middle-range bikes tend to be sports models. The Honda VF400 shown above has the appearance of a Grand Prix racer.

It has a four-cylinder, liquid-cooled engine. Built around a tubular racing frame, the bike has other race-bred features. It has covered disc brakes, front and rear, and anti-dive front forks. These keep the front wheel steady during braking.

Big Bikes

In the superbike category, the K100 bikes are the biggest and best in the BMW range from Germany. Introduced in 1983, the K100 RS can move from 0–60 mph (0–100 k/hr) in 3.9 seconds and give a top speed of around 135 mph (215 k/hr).

The bike's power plant is a flat, four-cylinder engine. This is liquid cooled for noise reduction. Like all BMWs, the K100 has an enclosed shaft drive to the rear wheel.

BMW has done its best to produce a bike that is not only very fast but is also very safe at high speeds. Besides wind-tunnel tests, computer-aided design (CAD) has been used to calculate how the bike will stand up to stress. This is important, as many parts, including the engine, are made of light alloy. Laser beams are also used to check for faults before it leaves the factory.

Above: The Suzuki Katana.

Speed and Style
If you are looking for the collector's bike of the future, then the Katana is an obvious choice. The GSX1100S Katana is Suzuki's top model. It would be equally at home on the racing circuit or on the streets.

Speed and style is what the "Suzi" Katana is all about. It can cover one-quarter mile in 11.2 seconds from a standing start and has a top speed of around 140 mph (230 k/hr). The Katana's power comes from an air-cooled, direct overhead camshaft. It has a four-cylinder, four-stroke engine. There are four valves per cylinder – making sixteen in total. This gives smooth running at high speed.

The Katana's streamlining is definitely the shape of things to come. A streamlined fairing covers the front portion of the

bike. This improves wind resistance and offers the rider some protection from the weather. Cutting down on wind resistance not only increases rider comfort but also leads to improved performance and fuel economy.

As long ago as 1970, a British designer called Malcolm Newell built a bike that was totally enclosed in a streamlined body shell. His revolutionary new bike was called the Quasar.

Below: The latest in the BMW range – the fast and sporty K100 RS.

Classic Bikes

Above: The British Triumph
Bonneville took its name from the
650 cc special that set a new world
record of 224 mph (359.99 k/hr) at
Bonneville Salt Flats, Utah, in 1962.
The last Bonneville model rolled off
the Meriden production line in early
1983, when the company closed
down.

Below: The Italian company, Moto Guzzi, first introduced their race-bred Le Mans 850 in 1972. Like all Guzzi's bikes, it was streamline-tested in a wind tunnel. The result is a long, sleek racer. The latest model has one of the best braking systems around. It also has air-operated shock absorbers for greater stability.

Above: The 750 and 850 cc Norton Commando was the first new bike to be developed by Norton after they joined forces with the Villiers engine company in the late 1960s. It was a solid, high-performance bike with a vertical twin cylinder air-cooled engine. The Commando was popular in both the United States and Britain.

U.S. Style

Most American bikes are built for long-distance cruising. Harley Davidson's famous Electra Glide has a big 1340 cc engine. It is built for comfort and has fitted fairings.

The real Harley enthusiast, however, doesn't buy his machine ready-made – he customizes it. This is called "chopping."

The **chopper** shown below is based on a standard 1200 cc Harley. It has extra-long girder front forks – "Easy Rider" style. The rider's seat has been

lowered. The passenger sits up high on the back, and there is a specially-built, low-slung frame. Longer than the original, this custom-built frame gives the bike a "lean and hungry" look.

Tastes in customized bikes vary widely, however. In the chopper, all non-essential parts have been stripped away for speed. Some enthusiasts prefer to "dress" their bikes. The photograph below right also shows a 1200 cc Harley. It is buried beneath an impressive scaffolding of chrome **crashbars** and lights.

New Developments

**Below: The Honda CX500
Turbo. A 500 cc engine may
not seem very big, but its
turbocharger makes it equal
to 850 cc.**

Some of today's most advanced bikes are being fitted with turbochargers. A **turbocharger** is basically a turbine – a tiny propellor which has lots of curved fins. The turbine is fitted inside the engine's air intake pipe. As air passes through the pipe it turns the turbine. The moving turbine compresses the air and rams it toward the engine. Fuel is injected before the compressed air enters the cylinder.

A turbocharged engine has two big advantages. Firstly, it needs less gasoline than a normal engine. This is because fuel mixes more evenly with compressed air. Secondly, it gives more power and acceleration because the fuel/air mixture is forced into the engine at high pressure.

Turbocharging is not a new idea. In the 1930s, record-breaking racing bikes were fitted with simple compressors

Above: An experimental design for a new, highly streamlined motorcycle.

to blow air into their engines. But these bikes drank a lot of gasoline and they gave sudden and unexpected bursts of power.

Today's turbos have their fuel injection controlled by a tiny computer. The air intake is close enough to the exhaust to heat up the air that is entering the engine. In this way, a modern turbo bike saves fuel and gives up to 30 percent more power.

Shaped for Speed

Streamlining has become an important part of motorbike design. Like many changes, it owes it origins to the race track. As long ago as 1954, Moto Guzzi fitted a streamlined fair-ing over the front wheel of their 350 cc racing bike. The fairing reduced wind resistance and the bike won the World Championship. Other teams were quick to copy the idea.

Nowadays, we know more about **aerodynamics** – the study of objects moving through the air. Designs are now tested in wind tunnels to discover the best shapes for fairings. Touring bikes often have a full fairing that covers the headlight and handlebars and surrounds the rider's legs. On sports bikes, you are more likely to find a small, front fairing with a tiny windshield.

Lightweight Bikes

Not everyone wants a big bike. For short distances and city travel, scooters and mopeds have remained the ideal solution. Both Suzuki and Honda have improved on their original scooter designs. They now make a range of lightweight bikes that are aimed at the shopper.

The Honda Stream, shown below, is a three-wheeler. The two tiny back wheels give it stability. Its automatic transmission and electric starter make it one of the easiest bikes to ride. Steering is easy too. To turn, you simply lean over in the direction you want to go. Unlike a normal scooter, the Stream has built-in luggage space.

In years to come, we can expect new and unusual designs for small bikes. There will be foldaway scooters and maybe even tiny electric bikes that enclose the rider in a plastic bubble. Perhaps one day, small bikes will even run on solar energy.

Below: The new Honda Stream, one of the latest lightweight bikes.

Racing

One of the most famous bike races in the world is the Tour de France. Founded in 1903, by Henri Desgrange, the route covers about 2,400 miles (3,860 km). It is the world's longest cycle race. The start is at Charleroi in Belgium and the finish is at Paris. In between, the route winds around most of France, including two high mountain ranges – the Pyrenees and the Alps. It is a real test of endurance for the riders.

The race is divided into 21 stages. Each stage is a day's cycling and riders eat and drink on the move. The only rest comes at the end of the day's run. Competitors ride in teams. Each team will have a top rider. The others form a pack around him to protect him from attacks by other teams. Believe it or not, there is nothing in the rules to prevent cyclists cutting in front of each other. Sometimes the victim of such an attack can be forced off the road.

Team members will also help their top rider by changing bikes if he gets a puncture. When he needs to eat or drink, another rider will stop to pick up the food satchel and water bottle. He will sprint to catch

up with the leader and then fall back when the food and water have been handed over.

Crowds of people watch the race and the riders are followed by a convoy of vans carrying journalists, race officials, doctors, team managers and mechanics. There is a lot of excitement along the way. Every day there are prizes for the fastest time, or the best effort,

**Above: The Tour de France
is a grueling test of
endurance that lasts three
weeks.**

or even for plain bad luck!

The toughest test of all is the
Alps, where the route climbs to
nearly 7,000 feet (2,000 m)
above sea level. The riders have
to gasp for breath because the
air is very thin at this height.

On the downhill run the pace
is frightening. The leaders of
the race can be riding at speeds
of more than 50 mph (80 k/hr).
The last stages of the three-
week race are tough. The riders
are exhausted and the one with
the most staying power will be
the winner.

The winner will collect nearly
$150,000 in prize money. But he
will not keep it all. Every
member of the team will get a
share.

77

BMX Action

Above: A rider goes for "full speed."

Bicycle Motocross – BMX for short – is one of the fastest-growing new sports around. There are races throughout the country and international events. A lot of young people are beginning to take BMX very seriously.

The skill of **BMX** racing is getting to know your bike and what you can do with it. Beginners usually buy a **BMX** bike ready-made. The experts often prefer to make up their own bike from different parts.

These competition bikes are built to win races. A typical BMX track is a twisting, down-hill course with steep, banked corners and high bumps. The track starts off wide but soon narrows. Normally, there are eight riders in a race so it is vital to get off to a good start.

The course tests both rider and bike. Racing bikes have to stand up to rough riding. Their chrome moly (extra strong steel) frames are welded for lightness and strength. The wheels, too, have to be extra strong. "Mag" (magnesium alloy) wheels are unlikely to bend, but spoked wheels on a strengthened rim are lighter. Racing wheels can be anything from 19–24 in (48–61 cm) and the fat tires have a heavy block tread for extra traction.

BMX bikes can move very fast – so fast that the front wheel sometimes wants to leave the ground. Racing frames are, therefore, made with a long, rear triangle and a steeply-angled seat pillar to shift the rider's weight towards the front. The balance of the bike makes it possible to do hair-raising tricks. The rider can actually raise the front end and do a "wheelie" simply by pulling up the handlebars. Ace

Above: Waiting for the "off," the riders sit with their feet poised on the pedals. The maximum number for a race is usually eight.

riders aim for "full air" when riding over "whoops," and some riders can even make their bikes jump over obstacles.

All these stunts add to the danger and thrill of **BMX**. Track racing is definitely not for the faint-hearted. With all the fast action and excitement, accidents can happen. A helmet and a mouthguard are a must, as are strong leather gloves and knee and elbow protectors.

Grand Prix

Motorcycle racing has a long and interesting history. One of the first international circuits was on the Isle of Man in the Irish Sea. The winding roads that circle the tiny island make an ideal race track. Steep hills and sharp bends add up to a circuit that can test even the toughest bike.

The island's first motorcycle race was held in 1907. Because it was open to riders from all over the world, the race was called the Tourist Trophy. English machines won both events.

The single-cylinder race was won by Charlie Collier on a Matchless, and the two-cylinder class by Rem (short for Rembrandt!) Fowler on a Norton.

Today, World Championship Grand Prix racing takes place in twelve countries: South Africa, France, Italy, West Germany, Spain, Austria, Yugoslavia, Holland, Belgium, Britain, Sweden and San Marino. There are five classes of race, from 50cc to sidecar championships. The riders who gain most points in their class become world champions.

Right: Freddie Spender, the winner of the 1983, 500 cc Grand Prix World Championship.

The Grand Prix circuits are tough, but modern 500 cc bikes are now so fast that they can average 115 mph (185 k/hr) per lap easily. Nowadays, Japanese bikes dominate the 500 cc class. One of the world's top bikes is the Suzuki RG500 Gamma. The Gamma's engine is a water-cooled two-stroke, with four cylinders arranged in a square. It has a power output of 130 hp, giving a top speed of around 160 mph (260 k/hr).

weight. Racing tires have no
tread. They are called **'slicks'**.
In wet weather, tires with a thin
parallel tread are used for road
holding.

The bikes that take part
in international Grand Prix

A typical racing bike is very
different from a road machine.
Besides full aerodynamic fairing, it will have a five or six-
speed gearbox, twin disc brakes
at the front and a single disc at
the rear. Most racing bikes have
a square-section frame made of
alloy. Alloy is a softer, lighter
metal than steel. The square
shape of the frame sections
gives it all the strength of
a tubular frame without the

races are special factory-built machines – "one offs." But there is another kind of racing – Formula or Production TT. Formula racing is for road machines, but special modifications are allowed. Besides careful engine tuning, Formula bikes are fitted with racing tires. All extras, like horn, lights, indicators and number plates, are removed. Riders are even allowed to fit a stronger crankshaft and an extra gear, provided that the power output stays the same.

The prize money makes Production racing very attractive to competitors and Honda rider, Joey Dunlop, won $15,000 in prize money when he won the Isle of Man Formula I TT in January 1983.

Below: A group of riders jostle for the lead at the 1981 Marlboro TT, at Brands Hatch.

Motocross and Scrambling

Motocross is a fast cross-country circuit event. Two-stroke bikes are used mainly because they are lighter and perform well. Riders have to be very fit. The exercise comes from handling the bike at speed over bumps, and controlling skids. When a bike jumps high in the air, the rider has to stand up and lean back. His weight will make sure that the back wheel lands first. The rider uses his whole body to control skids, and feet are used in cornering.

The World Motocross Championships are held in twelve rounds in twelve different countries and there are classes for 125, 250 and 500 cc bikes.

Youthclass Scrambling is an offshoot of Motocross. Riders can start at an early age – from six upwards. But there is a limit on the size of the bike these youngsters can ride. Anyone under eight can ride only 50 cc bikes, eight-to ten-years-old can ride up to 100 cc and teenage riders can ride anything up to 200 cc depending on their age.

Grass-track racing is also popular for young riders. The flat grass circuit is similar to a speedway track and the thrills come from taking corners in a controlled sideways skid.

Right: A rider takes to the air while negotiating a Motocross circuit.

Below: Youthclass scrambling is the best training for future adult riders.

Trials and Enduro

In the early days of motor-cycles, ordinary machines were tested by riding them up steep hills to see how powerful they were. Nowadays, special bikes are used for off-road trials riding.

A club trial takes place on very rough and hilly country. Riders can meet all sorts of hazards, from muddy tracks and mountain streams to rocks and boulders. A typical trial is 40 miles (60 km) long and there can be anything up to 60 sections, each judged by a team of marshals.

Most trials take place from November to March when the weather is at its worst. Riders lose marks for stopping and taking their foot off the footrest. The winner is the one who covers the ground in the best time and loses the least points.

Trials bikes are different from any other kind of bike. They have high, wide cowhorn handlebars, a short frame and block tread tires. They need a sturdy engine with a lot of **torque** (pulling power) for hill climbs. These are usually two-stroke engines. The engine is high up in the frame for added ground clearance. The suspension is extra high to cushion the hardest bumps.

Enduro racing is long-distance riding over country trails. Often the course is 100 miles (160 km) but it can be more. Enduro has none of the spectacular hill climbing and mud wallowing of a trials event, but it calls for a lot of skill nonetheless.

An Enduro race usually lasts for a day. All bikes have to be the same engine size and the object of the race is to be first past the winning post. The bikes start in pairs. Tracks can sometimes be very rough, and riders need to carry tools in order to make speedy trackside repairs. Broken chains, punctures and other breakages can and do happen.

Enduro, or trail bikes, can be bought for road use. Road machines will have softer shock absorbers and may not be as tough, but they are good enough for the purpose of most off-road riding.

Below: a Husqvarna Enduro bike. Note the very long front forks to absorb the bumps of a rough trail.

Stunt Riding

Motorcycle stunt riders can earn enormous sums of money. The fees for each performance are high and a top rider can earn enough to live comfortably even if he only makes one or two appearances a year. But the risk is equally high.

The most famous stunt rider of them all is Evel Knievel. In the course of his brief career he has broken nearly every bone in his body. But his daredevil stunts captured the imagination of the world. Many riders have tried to follow his lead.

Knievel's most daring stunt was the legendary leap across the Snake River Canyon. With rockets strapped to his bike and parachutes to provide a soft landing, the fearless stuntman gunned his Harley Davidson up a ramp and over the edge of the deep canyon. The rockets fired and took both man and motorcycle over the river foaming below. But the stunt went wrong when the parachutes opened too soon. Instead of reaching the other side of the canyon, his bike fell short. It was a long drop to the riverbank below and a long drive to the nearest hospital for emergency treatment.

Above: A rider from the Imps display team. All the riders are under sixteen.

Knievel has paid more than $50,000 in hospital bills and has survived 30 major crashes. He now walks with a permanent limp and his hip is held together by a steel plate. His last appearance was at Wembley Stadium in Britain, in May 1975.

Britain's Eddie Kidd has been luckier. So far, he has not had any major accidents. In September 1976, Kidd jumped over thirteen double decker buses. He cleared the buses but went out of control as he landed. He skidded into the crowd and injured two people.

Next year, Eddie Kidd was back – as a challenger in the World Target Jumping Championship. The crowds stood well back as he got ready for his first jump. He roared up the ramp and took off. He cleared 18 cars and landed perfectly. He jumped twice more, clearing 20 cars each time. At the fourth jump, Kidd cleared 22 cars and won the Championship. He had made a record leap of 126 feet (38.4 m).

Jumping over cars and buses is dangerous, but jumping over people is more so.

In September 1978, Kidd found ten volunteers for his most dangerous stunt ever. The volunteers were all radio disc jockeys and they were doing it to raise money for charity. The DJs had their lives insured for over a million dollars. One by one, the DJs lay down on the grass. Kidd raced up to the ramp and cleared the DJs with yards to spare.

Before he makes any of his death-defying leaps, Eddie Kidd always takes a bit of grease from the chain of his bike and dabs it on his heel. He says it is for good luck.

Below: Evel Knievel at Wembley, England. He managed to jump thirteen buses, but crashed on landing.

Glossary

Aerodynamics The study of the movement of an object through the air.

Alternator An electricity generator powered by an engine.

Camshaft The shaft which opens and closes the inlet and exhaust valves of an engine.

Carburetor The part of an engine where air is mixed with the gasoline before it is pumped into the cylinder. The mixture passes through a jet which turns it into a fine spray.

Chain wheel The toothed wheel that is turned by the pedals and which drives the chain on a bicycle.

Choke Controls the amount of air taken into the carburetor.

Chopper The name given to a bike which has been personally adapted.

Clutch The device which disconnects the main drive from the crankshaft, from the gears.

Compression As a piston moves upward it compresses or squeezes the gas/air mixture inside the cylinder.

Crankcase The part of the engine that contains the crankshaft.

Crankshaft The main shaft of an engine, which is turned by the pistons and which passes the movement on to the drive shaft or chain.

Crashbars Chrome-plated steel bars that protect a rider's legs.

Cylinder The closed tube that contains an engine's piston.

Derailleur A bicycle gear, in which the chain is moved across a set of differently-sized sprocket wheels.

Disc brake A brake which operates against a shiny metal disc attached to the hub of a bike's wheel.

Distributor Part of a bike's electrical system that divides or distributes the current between the spark plugs.

Drive chain The chain that transmits or carries the engine's power from the crankshaft to the rear wheel. (Instead of a drive shaft).

Drive shaft The shaft that transmits or carries the engine's power from the crankshaft to the rear wheel. (Instead of a drive chain.)

Drum brake See hub brake.

Enduro Long-distance trail race.

Exhaust The spent gases that are expelled from the cylinders of an engine.

Fairing The streamlined shield fitted to the front of a bike to reduce wind resistance.

Flat engine An engine where the

cylinders lie opposite one another across the body of the bike.

Flywheel A weighted wheel on the crankshaft that acts as a counterbalance to the pistons.

Front forks The metal struts that hold a bike's front axle.

Gearbox The case that encloses the gears of a motorcycle or automobile.

High-tension coil A device for boosting current from the battery to the distributor.

Hub The center of a wheel.

Hub brake Also called drum brake. A metal drum that fits over the hub of a wheel, containing two brake shoes that press against the drum wall to stop the wheel.

Hub gear See Sturmey Archer.

Ignition The electric current needed to fire the spark plug.

Motocross A short distance, cross-country scrambling event.

Muffler The device that cuts down the noise made by the exhaust.

Piston The part that moves up and down inside an engine's cylinders.

Pneumatic Air-filled.

Shock absorbers The coil springs and oil-filled dampers used to cushion a bike against bumps over an uneven surface.

Slicks Special racing tires.

Spark plug A device through which electricity passes. Inside the plug is a gap across which the electric current jumps to form a spark. This ignites the gas inside the cylinder.

Sprocket wheel Toothed gear wheel.

Sturmey Archer A bicycle gear, which is contained inside the hub of the rear wheel. When the gear is in position, a shaft which runs through the center of the hub, connects with one of three gear wheels.

Suspension The system of shock absorbers used on a bike's frame.

Throttle The device which controls the amount of fuel mixture entering the engine.

Torque The turning power of an engine.

Transmission The system of moving parts that conveys the engine's power to the rear wheel.

Turbocharger A fan for making compressed air to boost the engine.

Vee twin An engine with two cylinders laid out in the shape of a "V."

Index

Page numbers in *italics*
refer to illustrations.

A

Aerodynamics 74, 90
Alternator 43, *43,* 90
Ariel Square Four 54

B

Battery 43, *43*
Benz, Karl 17
Bernardi Enrico 24
Black Lightning 54
Bloomers *15*
BMW 51, 52, 55, 63, 66, *67*
BMX 78–79
Boneshaker 6, 10–11
Bonneville *68*
Bonneville Salt Flats 68
Boots 46, *47*
Bouton, Georges 20
Brakes 10, 31, *31,* 35, 37, *37,* 44–45, *44–45,* 69
Brando, Marlon 59
Brands Hatch 83
Briggs 23
Brough Superior 55
BSA *50*
Butler, Edward 18

C

C50 Moped 60, *62–63*
Camshaft 42, *42,* 52, 90
Canadian Cyclist Corps *49*
Carburettor 41, *41, 90*
Célérifère 8, *8*
Chain 26, *26,* 28, *28,* 32, *32,* 42, *42*
Chain wheel *26,* 28, 29, 90
Choke 37, 90
Chopper 70–71, *70–71,* 90
Christie, E. J. 24, *25*
Clothing *15,* 46–47, 79
Clutch 18, 40, 41, 42, *42,* 54, 90
Collier, Charlie 80
Compression 38, 39, 90
Commando *69*

Crankcase *38,* 39, *39,* 42, *42,* 90
Crankshaft 40, 41, *41,* 42, *42, 54, 90*
Crashbars 71, *71,* 90
Customized bikes 70–71, *70–71*
Cylinder 16, 38, 39, 41, *41,* 42, *42,* 51, 54, 90
CX500 Turbo *72–73*

D

Daimler, Gottlieb 16, 17, 18
D'Ascanio, Corrado 60
De Dion 19, 20
De Dion Bouton 20
Delivery bicycles 53, *53*
Derailleur 23, 26, 27, *27,* 28, 90
Desgrange, Henri 76
De Sivrac, Comte 8
Disc brake 44, *44,* 90
Dispatch rider 48, *48*
Distributor 43, *43,* 90
Douglas bike *48*
Draisienne 8, 9
Drive chain 40, 52, 90
Drive shaft 37, 40, 52, 90
Drum brake *see* Hub brake
Dunlop, Joey 83
Dunlop, John Boyd 22

E

Easy rider 70
Egerton, Hubert 20
Einspur 17, *16–17,* 18
Electra Glide 70
Electrics 36, 43, *43*
Enduro 87, 90
Enduro bike *see* Trail bike
Engines 11, *11,* 16, 17, 18, 19, 20, 21, 24, 37, 38–42, 51, 54, 60, 62, 64, 65, 66, 70, 73, 74, 81, 87
Exhaust 38–39, *38–39,* 90

F

Fairing 63, 66, 74, 90–91
Fernihough, Eric 55
Flat engine 51, 91
Flywheel 16, *38, 39,* 42, *42,* 91

Foldaway bikes 56, 61, 75
Formula racing 83
Four-stroke engine 19, 38–39, 42, *42*
Fowler, Rem 80
Frames *8,* 12, 18, 19, 20, 21, 26, 51, 54, 65, 71, 79, 87
Front forks 65, 70, *87,* 91

G

Gamma *see* RG500 Gamma
Gangs 50
Gear lever *23,* 27, 28, 54
Gearbox 23, *23,* 27, *27,* 28, 37, 40, 41, 42, *42,* 51, 52, 91
Gears 18, 23, *23,* 27–28, 40, 42, *42*
Gold Wing *36–37*
Grand Prix racing 80–83
Grass-track racing 84

H

Harley Davidson 21, 48, 70, 71, *70–71,* 88
Hastings, Teddy *21*
Hell's Angles 59
Helmets 46, *47,* 79
Henne, Ernst 54, 55
High-tension coil 43, 91
Highway Code 34, 35
High-wheeler 6, 12–13, *12–13*
Hildebrand 19
Hobby-horse 6, 8, 9, *9*
Honda *36–37,* 60, 62, *62–63,* 64, *64,* 65, *65,* *72–73,* 75, *75,* 80–81, 83
Hub *27,* 28, *28,* 91
Hub brake 44, 45, *45,* 91
Hub gear 23, *32,* 91
Husqvarna *87*
Hydraulic brake 44–45

I

Ignition 36, 43, 63, 91
Imps display team *88*
Indian 21, *21,* 23, *23,* 48
Isle of Man 52, 80, 83

J

Johnson 23

K
K100 RS 66, *67*
Katana 66, *66–67*
Kawasaki 62, *64,* 65
KE125 *64,* 65
Kidd, Eddie 88, 89
Knievel, Evel 88, *89*

L
Lambretta 60
Langen 16
Leathers 46, *47*
Le Mans 850 *68–69*
Lights 35
Lightweight bikes 75, *75*
Lindley 23
London to Brighton race 19

M
Maintenance 29–33
Marlboro TT *82–83*
Marvin, Lee 59
Matchless 80
Maybach, Wilhelm *17*
MB50 64, *64,* 65
Meriden 68
Michaux, Ernest 11
Michaux, Pierre 10, 11
Mono-wheel 24, *25*
Moped 60, *62–63,* 64, *64,* 75
Motocross 84, *84,* 85
Moto Guzzi 51, 52, 63, *69,* 74
Motorrad 18, 19
Moulton, Alex 61
Moulton bicycle 61, *61*
Muffler *36,* 91
Mummy tire *22*

N
Newell, Malcolm 67
Norton 48, 69, 80

O
Oil 32
Otto 16
Oversuit 46, *47*

P
Paintwork 32–33, *33*
Panzer Corps *57*
Pedals 10, 20, 23
Petrol cycle 19
Piaggio 60

Piston 16, 38–39, *38–39,* 41, 42, *42, 44,* 91
Pneumatic tire 6, 22, *22,* 91
Portable bicycle 61, *61*
Production TT racing *see* Formula racing
Puncture 30, *30*

Q
Quadricycle 14
Quasar 67

R
Racing 19, 48, 52, 62, 63, 74, 76–77, *76–77,* 78, 79, 80–83, 84, 86–87
Racing bikes 80–83
Raleigh *61*
RG500 Gamma 81
Road safety 34–35
Roadster 26–28
Roberts, Kenny *82*
Rover Safety Bicycle 15
Royal Enfield 48

S
Schoolboy scrambling 84, *84*
Scooter 60, *60–61,* 75, *75*
Scrambling 64, 84, *84*
Shaft drive 60
Shock absorbers 36, 54, 63, 69, 91
Sidecar 48, 49, *50,* 51, 56, *57,* 80
Signals 34–35
Slicks *82,* 91
Sociable tricycle *14*
Spark plug 38–39, 91
Speed records 54, 55, 68
Sports roadster 26, *26–27*
Sprocket wheel 28, *29,* 41, 91
Starley, James 15
Stream 75, *75*
Streamlining 66, 67, 69, 74, *74*
Stunt riding 88–89, *88–89*
Sturmey Archer 28, *28,* 91
Suspension 61, 91
Suzuki 42, 62, 66–67, 75, 82

T
Thomson, Robert 22
Throttle 18, 54, 91
Tires 22, *22,* 30, *30,* 54, 79, 82–83, 87
Torque 87, 91
Tour de France 76–77, *76–77*
Touring bike 64
Trail bike 86, *86*
Trailer cycle 24, *24–25*
Transmission 40–42, *40–42,* 91
Trails *21,* 48, 86, 87
Trials bike 86, *86*
Tricycles 14, *14,* 18, 19
Triumph 48, 63, *68*
TT races 52, 80, 83
Turbocharger 73–74, 91
Two-stroke engine 39, *39,* 62

V
Vee twin engine 21, 54, 91
Vélocifère 8
Vélocipède 10–11, 12
Vespa 60, *60–61*
VF400 65, *65*
Vincent HRD 54, *54–55*
Visor 46, *47*
Von Drais de Sauerbrunn, Baron 8

W
Werner 20, *20*
Wheels *8,* 9, 12, 22, *22,* 30, *30,* 61,.79
Wild One, The 58, 59
Wolfmüller 19
World Motocross Championships 84
World Target Jumping Championship 89
World War I 49
World War II 56, 58

Y
Yamaha 62
Youth Hostels 53